CW01508245

Good grief it's Maisie!

Written by Jane McGee
Illustrated by Mary Louise Simmons
Design by Gareth Simmons

Acknowledgements

Having an idea and turning it into a book is both challenging and rewarding.
I especially want to thank the individuals that helped make this happen.
Complete thanks to Mary Louise Simmons and Gareth Simmons for their fantastic illustrations.
Also, to Matt and Joe and of course Maisie.

This book is dedicated to Maisie

whose winning ways brighten the darkest of days.

This Book Belongs To Maisie

It was the best of times

Maisie and Keith were best friends.
Keith had been by Maisie's side from the time Maisie was a puppy.

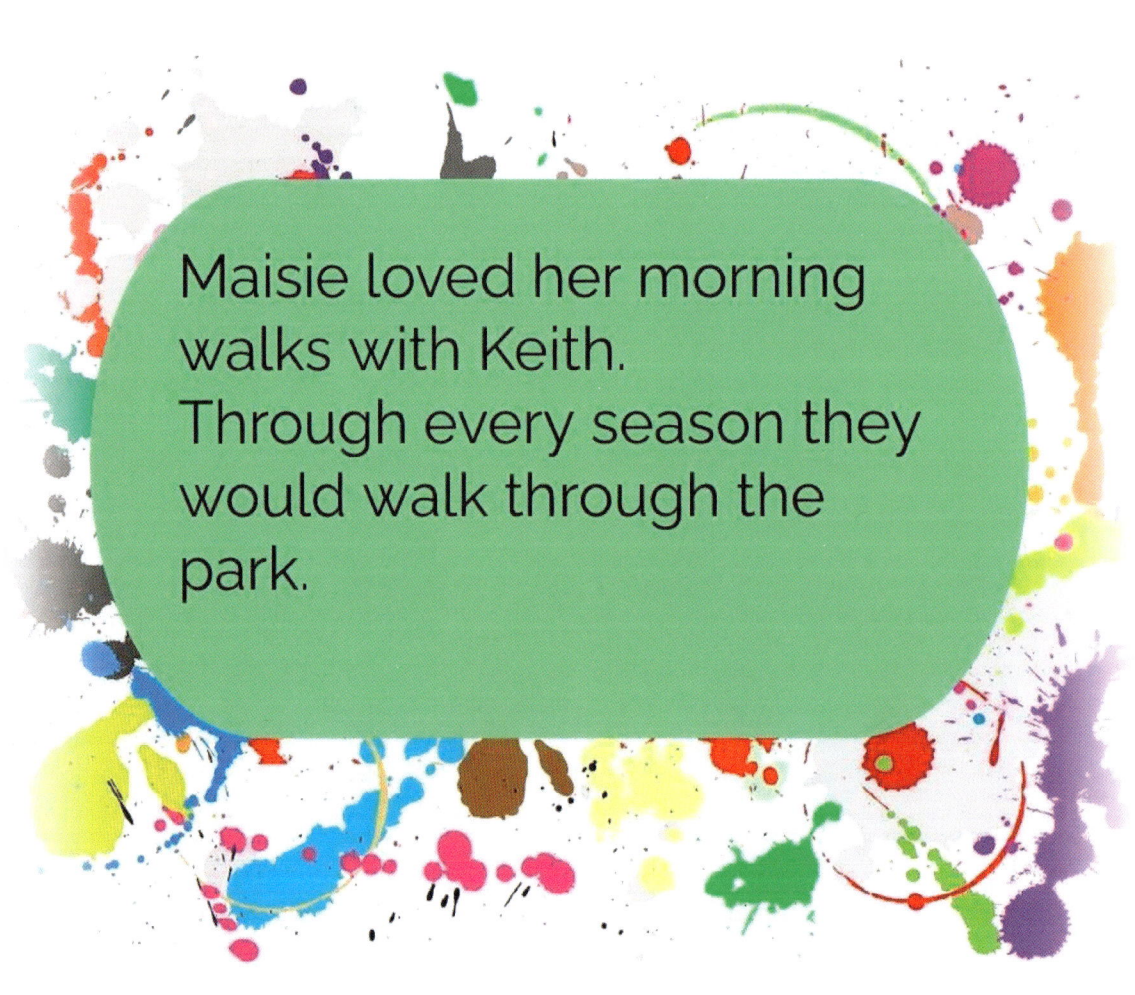

Maisie loved her morning walks with Keith. Through every season they would walk through the park.

In Spring

with the sweet smell of cherry blossom in the air, Maisie would chase the grey squirrels, who were always too quick for her.

In Summer

In the warm glow of the summer sun, Maisie would still try to catch the grey squirrels, who were still too quick for her.

In Autumn

The squirrels seemed to run even quicker in the autumn, as they searched for their acorns in the blanket of golden and yellow leaves on the ground.

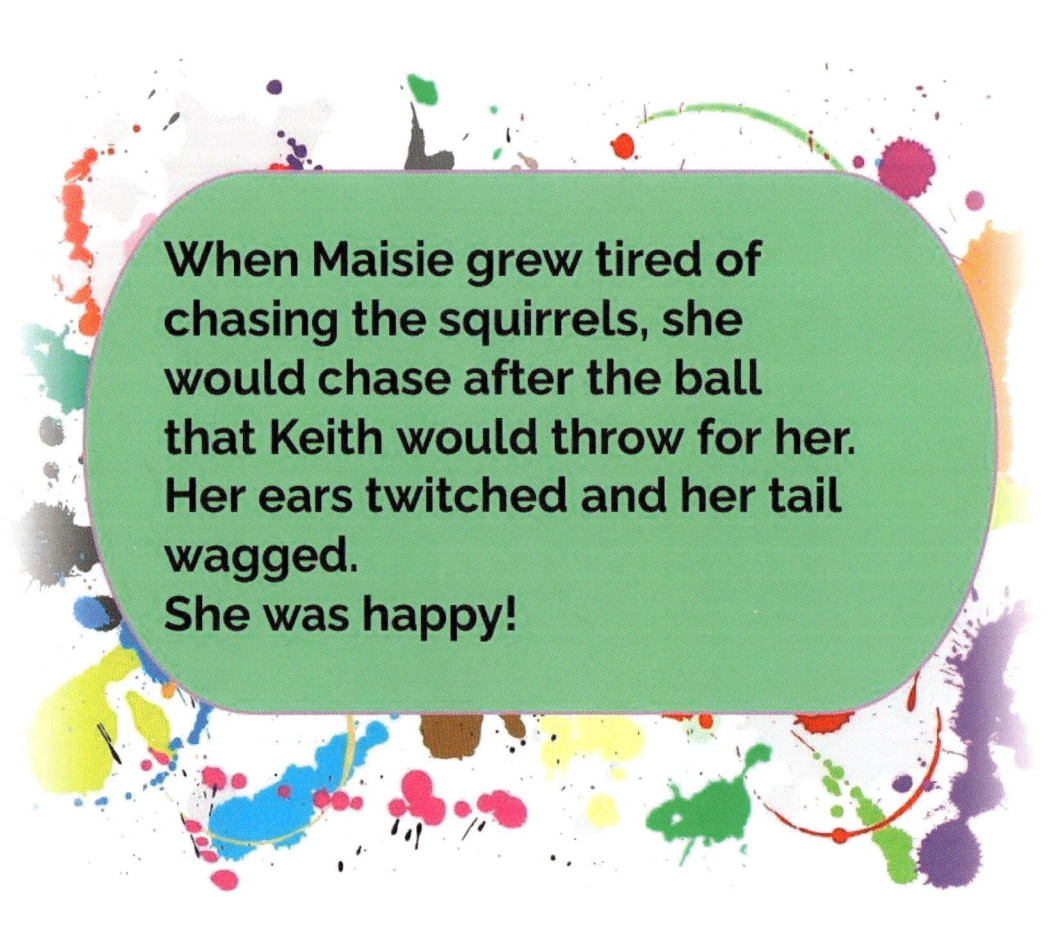

When Maisie grew tired of chasing the squirrels, she would chase after the ball that Keith would throw for her. Her ears twitched and her tail wagged.
She was happy!

Even better were her evening walks with Keith.
Every evening Maisie and Keith would walk along the river and then call in at the 'Dragon Inn' for something to drink and eat.

In the summer

Maisie would sit with Keith in the Dragon Inn garden.
The sun-sparkled butterflies waltzed around the honeysuckle.
The honey bees buzzed in the warm summer air.

In the Winter

Keith and Maisie would sit inside the Dragon Inn by the roaring log fire. Candles would flicker and Keith and Maisie would always receive a warm welcome from Matt and Joe, the Innkeepers.
Maisie would stare at the fiery flickering flames, wagging her tail and twitching her ears.

It felt like the good times
would never end and Keith and Maisie
would be best friends

forever

It was the worst of times

One morning in June, the clouds tumbled away and the golden summer sun rose and shone in through the window.

Maisie waited for Keith to take her for her early morning walk.

Keith would wake up soon.

Maisie would have her breakfast and they would go out for their walk through the park as they always did.

But Keith did not wake up

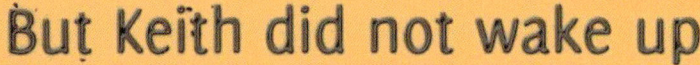

Keith had gone to sleep forever.
Maisie was lonely, sad, confused and
frightened.

The outside world was bursting with so
much colour, outside there was so much
wonder but inside something was not
right.

Maisie barked loudly all day
to wake Keith.

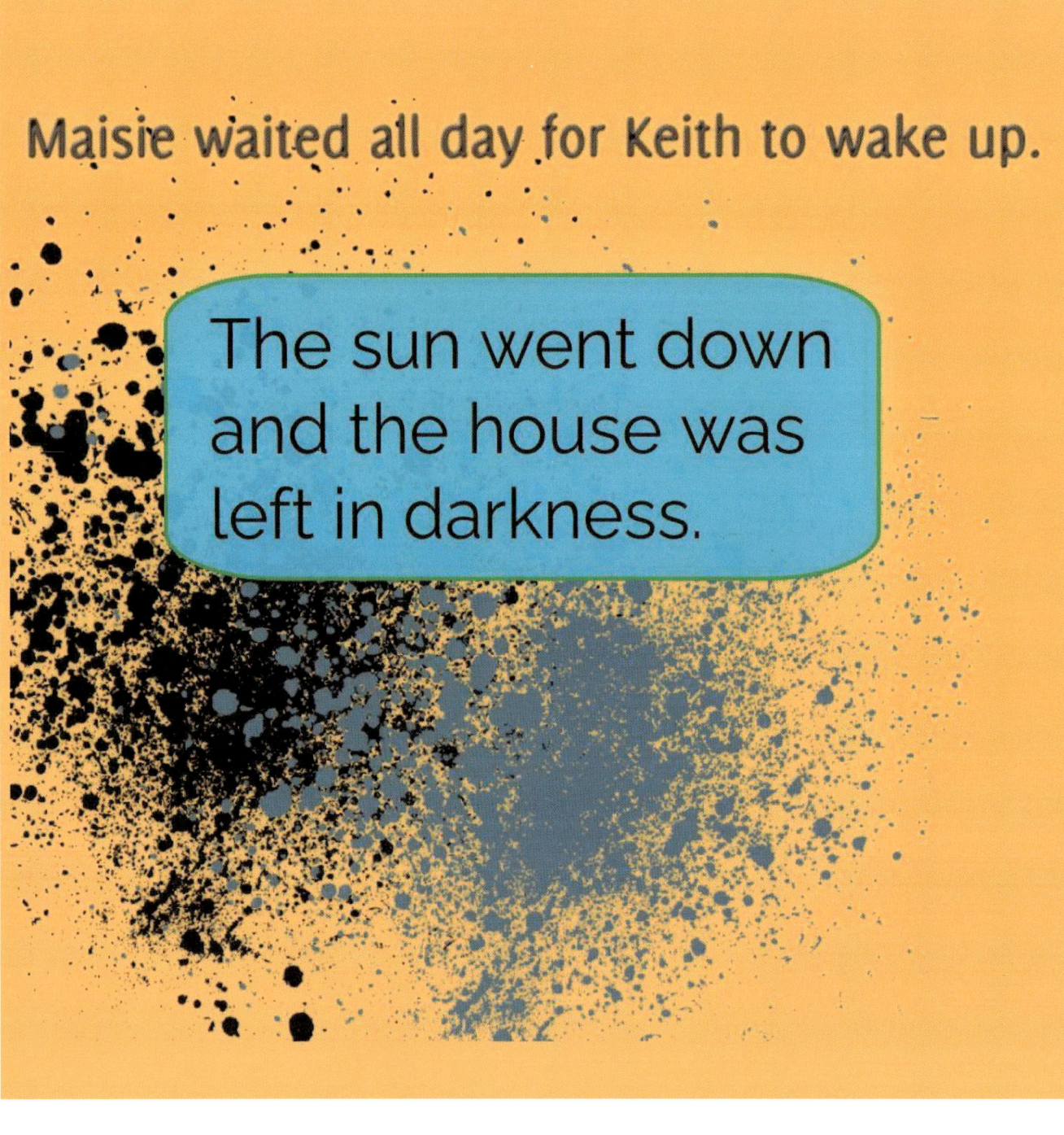

Maisie waited all day for Keith to wake up.

The sun went down and the house was left in darkness.

The next morning, Maisie looked out of the window as the sun rose.

A robin was sitting on the window. Keith loved robins and called them the 'Oak Kings of Summer.'

Maisie looked at the robin and the robin looked back at Maisie.

It opened its beak and let out a merry tune.

The robin stayed for a while and then flew off into the bright June sunshine.

Maisie watched it fly high into the sky and then saw it fade from view into the clouds.

The Spring of Hope

All living things grow and flourish but then they eventually die.

Keith had gone but Maisie had found a new home.

It was 'The Dragon Inn.'

Maisie wagged her tail and twitched her ears, then ran inside to the chair by the fire, where Keith used to sit on the cold winter evenings.

But the chair was empty.

She then ran outside to the chair by the honeysuckle trees, where she and Keith would sit on the warm summer evenings.

The chair was empty, Keith was not there.

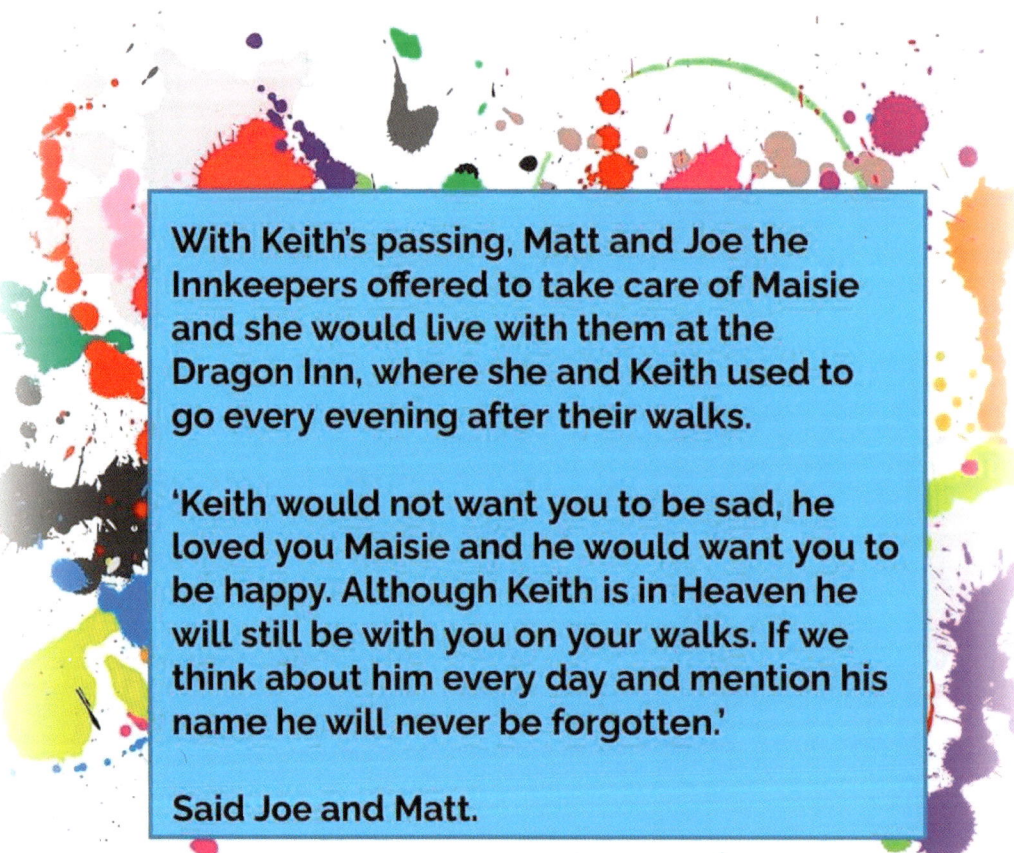

With Keith's passing, Matt and Joe the Innkeepers offered to take care of Maisie and she would live with them at the Dragon Inn, where she and Keith used to go every evening after their walks.

'Keith would not want you to be sad, he loved you Maisie and he would want you to be happy. Although Keith is in Heaven he will still be with you on your walks. If we think about him every day and mention his name he will never be forgotten.'

Said Joe and Matt.

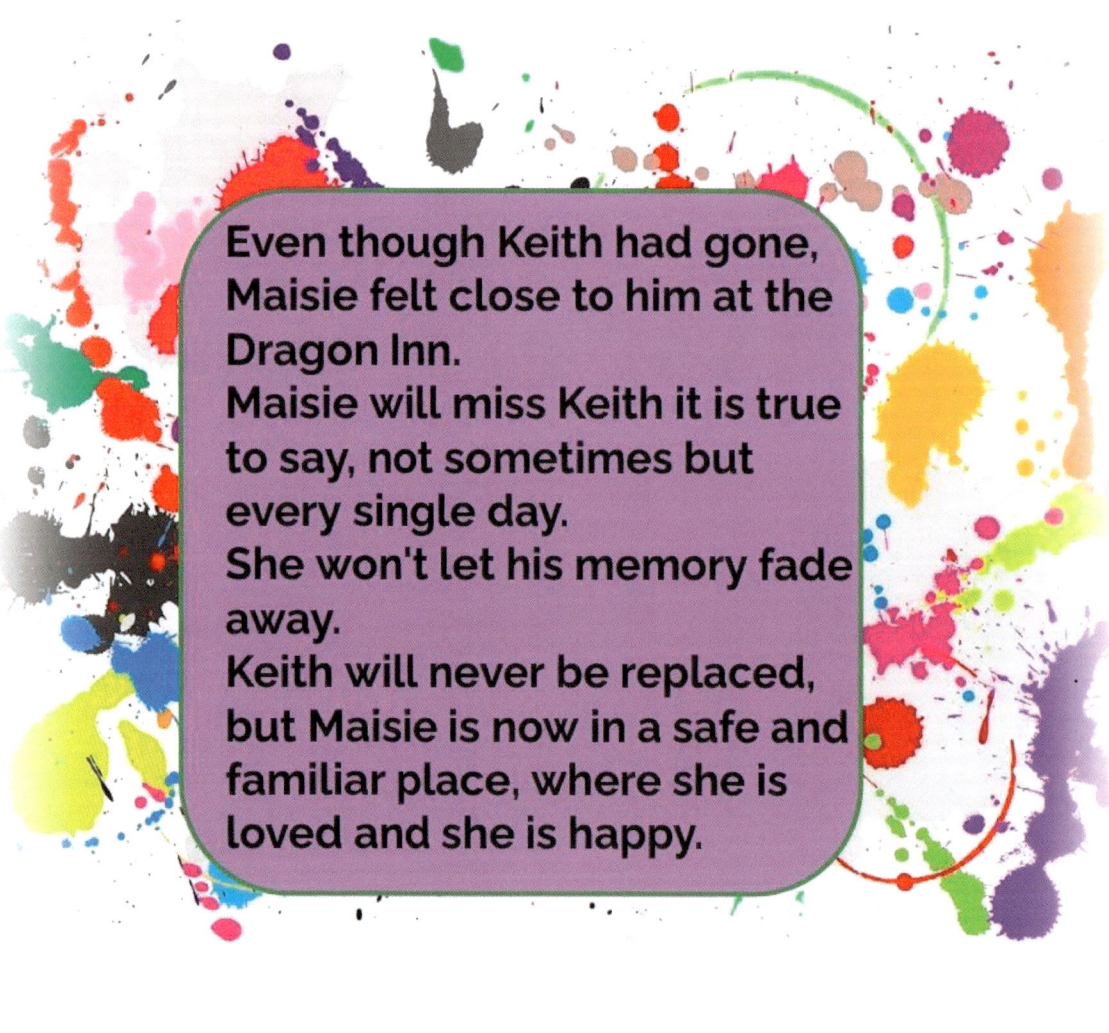

Even though Keith had gone, Maisie felt close to him at the Dragon Inn.
Maisie will miss Keith it is true to say, not sometimes but every single day.
She won't let his memory fade away.
Keith will never be replaced, but Maisie is now in a safe and familiar place, where she is loved and she is happy.

The author

Jane McGee works as a teacher and is passionate about wildlife and conservation.

She has written books about spiders, Adders and George the Stourbridge Station Cat.

All of her books donate their profits to charity.

Find out more about her work at

www.cobwebcapers.com

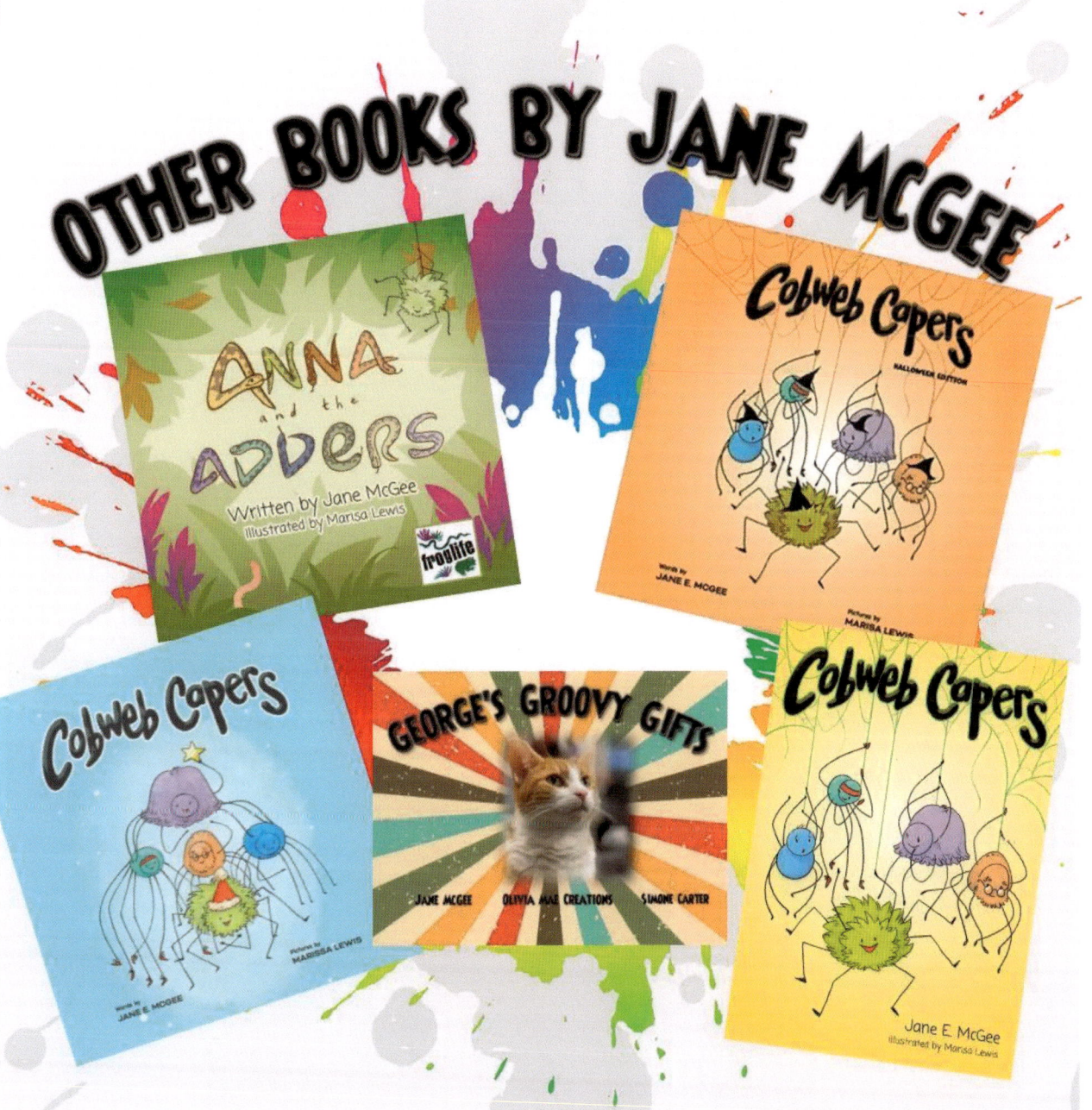

OTHER BOOKS BY JANE MCGEE

The Illustrator

The artist is a transplanted New Yorker, now living in
Colorado Springs, with her family and where she founded Scottish
Terrier Rescue of Colorado Springs. Many of her art prints are donated
to help support other animal causes. Her art has sold on many of the
Colorado PBS art auctions. She has made three appearances, on Good
Morning Colorado, talking about animal issues. The artist, asks children,
to be kind to animals at all times, for they have feelings too. Check out
her work at: www.lulu.com and
www.scottishterrierartprintscom.weebly.com

The graphic designer

Gareth Simmons, is an artist in the fields of oil and acrylic painting, graphic design, clay sculpting and photography.
www.zazzle.com/garethstore.
www.lulu.com

Owning a Miniature Schnauzer

Pros	Cons
Loyal	Bark a lot
Smart	Need mental stimulation
Adaptive	High maintenance
Easy to train	Heart issues
No shedding	Suffer from genetic illness

Dealing with grief

You are not alone

It's okay to be angry and to express your anger

It's OK to feel nothing

Don't feel guilty for having fun

It's okay to reach out for help

There is no one way to grieve

It's okay not to be okay.

Take the next step, the next minute, the next day, one at a time

Activity time

How to draw a Schnauzer

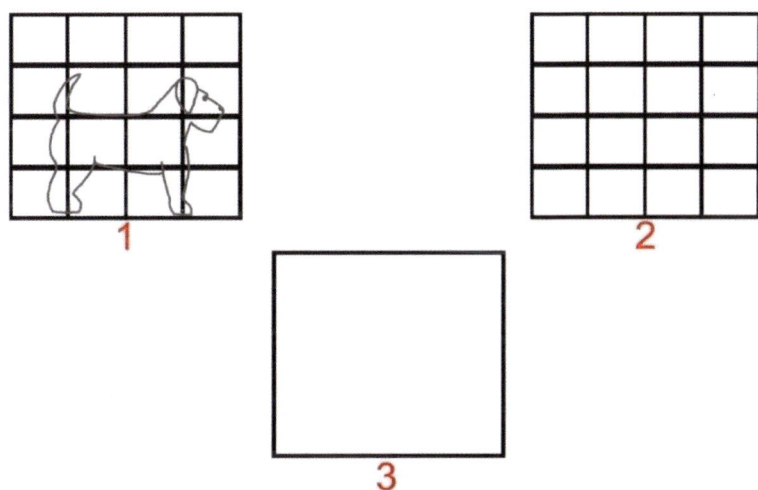

1

2

3

Copy the drawing into square 2 and then draw your image in square 3.

Amazing Maisie.

START

Can you help Maisie find her ball?

Amazing Maisie answer.

Can you find Maisie in this image?

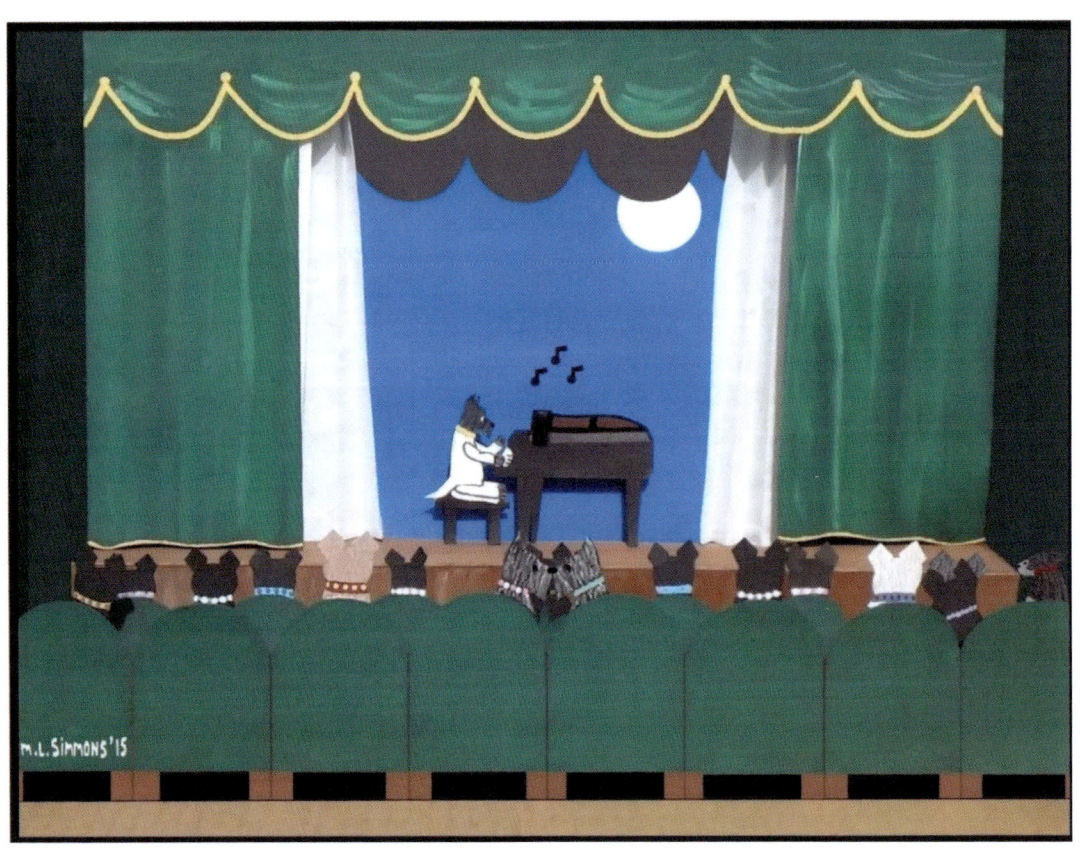

Did you find Maisie in this image?

Can you sort the Scotties from the Schnauzers?

SCHNAUZER

SCOTTIE

Maisie has floppy ears.

Scottie has pointed ears.

ICE CREAM

M.L. Simmons '18

There are 6 Schnauzers hiding in this picture.
Clue: one is very tiny!

Can you sort the Scotties from the Schnauzers?

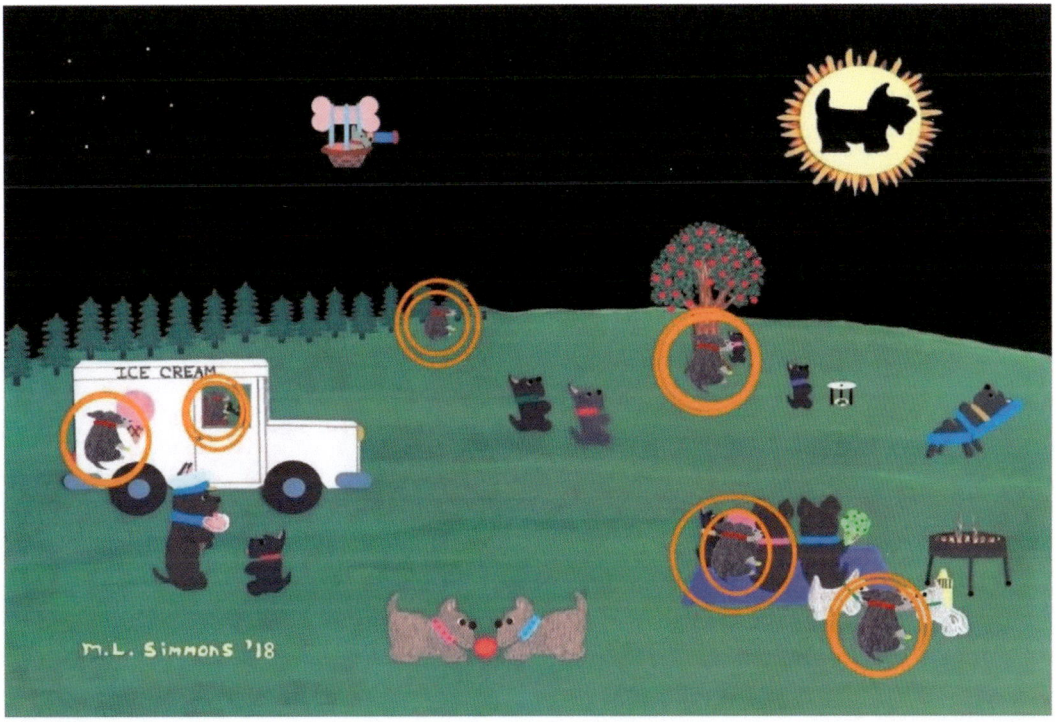

Here are the 6 Schnauzers. Did you spot them all?

Charities helped by the sale of this book

Winston's Wish is a childhood bereavement charity in the UK. The charity offers a wide range of practical support and guidance to bereaved children, their families and professionals. The charity currently supports 40,000 bereaved children and young people per year.
For more information visit: https://www.winstonswish.org

Birch Hill Dog Rescue rescue dogs of all breeds and offer them a second chance of a loving new life.
It was first set up back in 1996. Birch Hill Dog Rescue has always offered unwanted, abandoned and neglected dogs the very best of care. It became a registered charity in 2010.

Over the years Birch Hill Dog Rescue has provided a bright light for dogs when all but hope had faded.

Read about their amazing work and ways in which you can support them at: https://birchhilldogrescue.org.uk

'Waiting'
by Mary Louise Simmons.
Available to purchase
at:

https://www.zazzle.com/
waiting_with_maisie_poster
-256850698071224458

10% from the sale of this image
will be donated to a
US Schnauzer
rescue!

If you like this book
please leave Maisie
a review on Amazon.

Printed in Great Britain
by Amazon

32932658R00034